Hello, Puddle!

By Anita Sanchez · Illustrated by Luisa Uribe

CLARION BOOKS
An Imprint of HarperCollinsPublishers
Boston   New York

This book is dedicated to all puddle-lovers, no matter how many legs they have –A.S.

For Francisco, who always knows where the best puddles are –L.U.

Clarion Books is an imprint of HarperCollins Publishers.

Hello, Puddle

clarionbooks.com

The illustrations in this book were done in Adobe Photoshop while looking out the window.

The text was set in Tropen.

Cover and interior design by Celeste Knudsen

Library of Congress Cataloging-in-Publication Data is on file.

ISBN: 978-0-358-38144-0

Manufactured in Italy

ROTOLITO SPA 10 9 8 7 6 5 4 3 2 1

4500841734

First Edition

Hello, puddle!

Who's here?

Tadpoles wriggle and squiggle.

Toad eggs will hatch in a few days, and tadpoles will quickly turn into tiny toadlets.

Seeds take root.

Grasses, wildflowers, and tree
seedlings soak up water, sending
out leaves and roots.

Swallows loop the loop.

Barn swallows grab a beakful of mud. They'll raise their babies in a dried-mud cradle.

Mother turtle scratches and digs.

A female turtle needs soft soil to dig a hole and lay eggs. Warmed by the sun, baby turtles will hatch out weeks after she's back in the pond.

Ducklings nibble.

Ducks scoop up puddle water with their
beaks to strain out tiny bugs and plants.

Snails make tracks.

Moist, slimy skin helps snails
soak up air to breathe.

Mother wasp scoops and rolls.

A mud dauber wasp rolls tiny mud balls.
She'll carry the mud to a rock or wall, then
craft a sturdy house to shelter her eggs.

Robins dip and splash.

Birds love a good bath. Clean feathers help them fly their best when it's time to find food—or dodge a predator!

Mosquitoes hatch—
hungry bats swoop!

Mosquitoes lay eggs in still water. When the eggs hatch and turn into grown-up insects, it's time for bats to grab a tasty meal. One bat can eat a thousand mosquitoes a night!

Squirrels keep cool.

Summer can be hot, especially
when you've got a fur coat!

Puddle shrinks in summer heat.

Smaller . . .

smaller . . .

smaller . . .

Rain!

Butterflies feast.

Butterflies uncoil long
tongues to feed on minerals
found in damp soil. This is
called "puddling."

Deer silently sip.

Thirsty deer stop by for a quick drink.
It might be a long way to a stream, so
they drink wherever they can.

Winter's on its way.

Goodbye,
puddle.

See you in the spring!

Author's Note

The puddle in this book is a real one: it's at the end of the long, sloping driveway that leads to my house. I've decided not to pave the driveway because I love puddle-watching! I've seen all the animals in this book in or near the puddle. Sometimes it dries up, but I always love to greet it again after a rain.

Welcome Puddles

A puddle is much more than a wet spot in the dirt. Puddles are homes, bathtubs, and drinking fountains for wildlife. They also provide a key ingredient for animal homes: mud!

Puddles can be anywhere—a schoolyard, a forest, or a city park. Even a tiny puddle the size of a saucer can be a spot for small creatures to dive in.

Deeper puddles are breeding places for toads, salamanders, or insects. Shallow puddles thick with mud aren't as good for bathing or drinking, but they provide sturdy building material for birds or wasps. And some puddles, like the one in this book, have enough water for splashing as well as plenty of mud around the edges.

Backyards used to be perfect places for puddles. Now most roads and driveways are paved, and lawns cover up much of the soil where puddles used to form—puddles filled with fresh rainwater, surrounded by lots of nice, clean mud!

Clean mud? Mud might be gooey and make your fingers or toes dirty, but it's just soil that has gotten wet.

But not every puddle is a clean puddle. Animals can be harmed or even killed by puddles that have oil, chemicals, or soap floating in them. If you scrub your dog with flea soap, or wash the car, or spray the lawn with weed killer, that can create puddles. But those are no place for animals to drink—or for you to splash in.

Make Your Own Puddle

During a drought, even tiny sources of water can mean the difference between life and death for small animals! Work with an adult to find ways to create your own puddles.

- Put a shallow dish or pie pan on the ground and fill it with small stones or marbles. Add water for an instant puddle! The stones will help keep small insects from drowning.

- Buy or make a birdbath from a shallow dish, and watch the birds have fun. Change the water every few days to keep it clean and fresh for the birds, and to discourage mosquitoes.

- If possible, consider leaving a hose dripping for a little while each day. Thirsty birds will often spot moving water and come to investigate.

- Find a spot of bare ground and pour a pitcher of water on it once a day. The mud this creates can provide a snack for butterflies.

Watching Wildlife

Water is like a magnet for living things. If you want to see wildlife, keep an eye out for puddles! You may also spy some of these clues that you've had animal visitors.

- See any wavy lines traced in the mud? Sometimes snails or slugs wander along the edges of puddles, leaving long trails behind.

- Look into the water–is anything moving? Little wrigglers might be mosquito larvae. Tadpoles are shaped like tiny spoons, with round heads and flat tails. Long-legged water strider insects might skate on the water's surface.

- Any footprints? Search for squirrel, deer, or rabbit tracks in the soft soil near puddles. People leave tracks, too!

- See small clumps of puddle mud stuck high on a wall? Mud dauber wasps need a place to nest, but leave them alone and they won't bother you.

Puddle Lovers

American toad (*Anaxyrus americanus*) Toads lay eggs in shallow pools, and the tadpoles zip through the process of metamorphosis. For some species of frogs, developing from egg to adult can take years, but toads do it all in a few weeks. There's no time to waste—they have to get a move on before their puddle vanishes and leaves them high and dry.

Plants All plants need water, but some types of plants especially like to have "wet feet." Willows, cattails, and cottonwood trees are just some of the plants that need wet soil to start growing.

Barn swallow (*Hirundo rustica*) I love to watch barn swallows dart and soar. These beautiful birds are creatures of the sky, but they can't survive without mud—no mud, no nests for their babies. It might take a pair of barn swallows hundreds of trips to a puddle to collect enough mud for one nest!

Snapping turtle (*Chelydra serpentina*) In early summer, female turtles leave their pond to lay eggs on land. They're very fussy and will sometimes walk a mile or more to find the right patch of soil—not too wet, not too dry, and soft enough to dig.

Wood duck (*Aix sponsa*) Wood ducks are "dabbling ducks" that feed in shallow water. Mother ducks don't carry food to their babies—they just show them where and how to look for food, and the ducklings soon catch on.

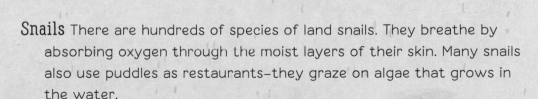

Snails There are hundreds of species of land snails. They breathe by absorbing oxygen through the moist layers of their skin. Many snails also use puddles as restaurants—they graze on algae that grows in the water.

Mud dauber wasp (*Sceliphron caementarium*) The black-and-yellow mud dauber wasp often chooses the side of a building as a place for her nest. The female attaches sticky mud to the wall while the male stands guard. Then she hunts for small spiders, which she puts inside the nest for the young to eat when they hatch! These wasps are not aggressive and are unlikely to sting people.

American robin (*Turdus migratorius*) A robin splashing in a puddle on a hot day seems to be having a blast! But the bird isn't doing it just for fun, or to cool off—keeping feathers clean is important for flying. Bathing can also help keep a bird's skin free from germs and infections, just as taking a bath does for you.

Mosquitoes (Culicidae spp.) Mosquito mothers bite you to feed on proteins in your blood that they need to create lots of eggs. When mosquito larvae hatch, they're about the size of this comma (,)—but they grow fast and are ready to metamorphose into adults in just a few days. Fortunately, mosquitoes are the favorite food of the . . .

Little brown bat (*Myotis lucifugus*) Little brown bats catch bugs in flight, then swoop low over a puddle to lick up a sip of water with tiny tongues. It may take dozens of trips back and forth over the puddle to get a good drink.

Gray squirrel (*Sciurus carolinensis*) You can meet these furry acrobats in wild forests or downtown parks. They often drink at puddles, but they can also get moisture from the leaves or fruits they eat.

Monarch butterfly (*Danaus plexippus*) Many types of butterflies, including monarchs, love puddles. Monarchs have a huge journey ahead—their fall migration can be thousands of miles—so they need lots of nutrition. Minerals from wet soil help power their long flight.

White-tailed deer (*Odocoileus virginianus*) Deer often leave their heart-shaped footprints near water. They lower their heads to take brief sips, then quickly look up and around for signs of danger.

Glossary

Absorb—to take in or soak up something, usually a liquid.

Drought—a time of dry weather, when an area gets less than the normal amount of rain.

Habitat—the home of an animal, where it can find food, water, and shelter, as well as a place to raise its young.

Larva—a stage between egg and adult in the lives of some kinds of animals that undergo metamorphosis. If there's more than one, they're called *larvae*.

Metamorphosis—the process of changing from one life stage to another. Frogs and many insects metamorphose from a larva that lives in water to an adult that lives on land.

Mineral—a chemical, like calcium or magnesium, often contained in soil.

Predator—an animal that hunts and feeds on other animals.

Puddling—a behavior of butterflies and other animals in which they suck nutrients from wet soil.

Seedling—a plant that has started to grow, with roots and baby leaves thrusting out of the seed.

Toadlet—a young toad that has just finished changing from a tadpole into an adult. When toadlets first leave the water, they're about half an inch long.

Learn More!

Books

Peterson Field Guides for Young Naturalists. Published by Houghton Mifflin Harcourt. A series of books to help you identify common backyard birds and insects. www.hmhbooks.com/series/peterson-field-guides-young-naturalists

Wait Till It Gets Dark: A Kid's Guide to Exploring the Night. By Anita Sanchez and George Steele, published by Globe Pequot, 2017. Learn more about bats, mosquitoes, deer, and other animals.

Online

- Check out the website of the **National Wildlife Federation** for ways to create a backyard or schoolyard habitat for wildlife. **www.nwf.org**

- Go to the website of the **Cornell Laboratory of Ornithology** and check out their Live Cams to see barn swallows, robins, and other birds nesting, drinking, and bathing. **www.allaboutbirds.org**

- Head over to the website of the **National Audubon Society** to learn about backyard bird counts and other ways to participate in citizen science. **www.audubon.org**

Bibliography

Burkett-Cadena, Nathan. *Mosquitoes of the Southeastern United States.* Tuscaloosa, AL: University of Alabama Press, 2013.

Gibbs, James P., and Alvin R. Breisch. *The Amphibians and Reptiles of New York State: Identification, Natural History, and Conservation.* New York: Oxford University Press, 2007.

Gullen, P. J., and P. S. Cranston. *The Insects: An Outline of Entomology,* 4th ed. Hoboken, NJ: Blackwell Publishing, 2010.

Long, Kim. *Frogs: A Wildlife Handbook.* Boulder, CO: Johnson Books, 1999.

Papoulis, Dimitrios, et al. "Mineralogical and Textural Characteristics of Nest Building Geomaterials Used by Three Sympatric Mud-nesting Hirundine Species." *Scientific Reports* 8 (July 23, 2018). (www.nature.com/articles/s41598-018-29307-8)

Smith, Joe. "Splish, Splash: Why Do Birds Take Baths?" *Cool Green Science.* March 9, 2015. (blog.nature.org/science/2015/03/09/backyard-bird-baths-science-birding-wildlife-habitat)

Thomas, S. A., Y. Lee, M. A. Kost, and D. A. Albert. Abstract for vernal pool. Lansing, MI: Michigan Natural Features Inventory, 2010.